Rookie Read-About® Science

It Could Still Be a Worm

By Allan Fowler

Consultants
Robert L. Hillerich, Professor Emeritus,
Bowling Green State University, Bowling Green, Ohio;
Consultant, Pinellas County Schools, Florida

Lynne Kepler, Educational Consultant

Fay Robinson, Child Development Specialist

Children's Press ®
A Division of Grolier Publishing
New York   London   Hong Kong   Sydney
Danbury, Connecticut

Project Editor: Downing Publishing Services
Designer: Herman Adler Design Group
Photo Researcher: Feldman & Associates, Inc.

Library of Congress Cataloging-in-Publication Data

Fowler, Allan.
    It could still be a worm / by Allan Fowler.
      p. cm. – (Rookie read-about science)
    Includes index.
    Summary: A simple introduction to the earthworm, roundworm,
flatworm, and other kinds of worms.
    ISBN 0-516-06052-X (lib. bdg.) - ISBN 0-516-20217-0 (pbk.)
    1. Worms—Juvenile literature. [1. Worms.] I. Title. II. Series.
QL386.6.F68   1996   95-39675
                                          CIP
                                          AC

How long is a worm? About as long as this worm — if it's a common earthworm, the kind you usually find in gardens.

earthworm

A really big earthworm
might reach from the
top to the bottom of
this book.

Some are even longer
than that.

When you look closely
at an earthworm, you see
that its body is made up of
many rings, or segments.

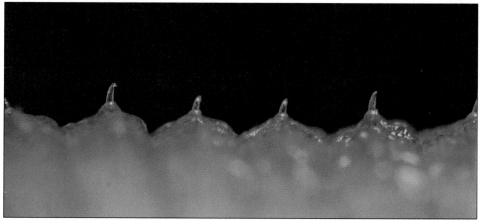

It moves with the help of hairs
like the bristles on a brush.

A worm could be much, much smaller than an earthworm, and still be a worm.

European corn borer

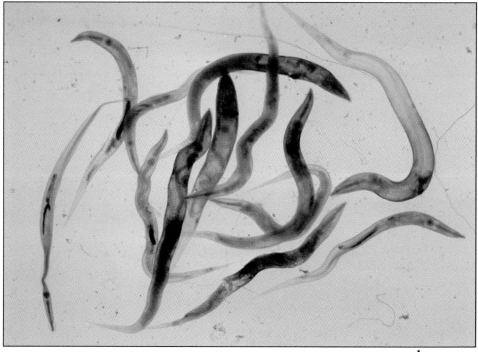

roundworms

Some roundworms are so tiny that a hundred of them could stretch out, end to end, on this line. _____

Or a worm could
be longer than an
automobile and
still be a worm —
like this giant
Australian earthworm.

A small farm might have more worms than a big city has people.

You wouldn't see most of them, because they spend so much time underground.

Worms make tunnels in the earth called burrows.

Earthworms that come out of their burrows after dark are called night crawlers.

People who go fishing
in lakes or rivers often
use night crawlers to
attract the fish.

Not all worms live in the
earth. A worm could live
in the sand along a beach,

or swim in the ocean . . .
and still be a worm — a sea
worm or a ribbon worm.

Not all worms have
dull colors.

A worm could be bright
red, orange, or blue . . .
and still be a worm —
like this ribbon worm.

Some ribbon worms are
no more than one inch,
but others are the longest
of all worms.

17

A worm could have a flat
body and still be a worm
— a flatworm.

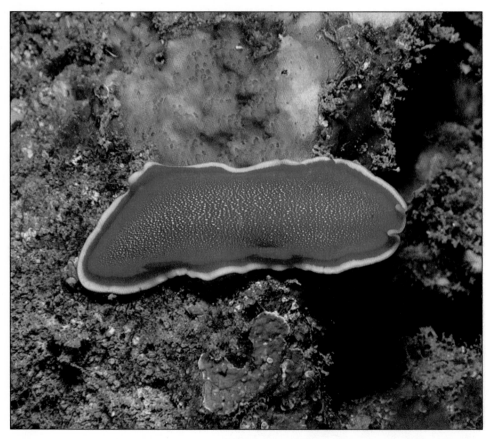

Here's an amazing fact about flatworms, ribbon worms, and some kinds of earthworms:

If they are cut into two or more pieces, each piece can live by itself as a whole worm.

But please — don't go around cutting up worms!

There are many thousands
of kinds of worms.

Worms are not insects.

Some animals that look
like worms are really
young insects that
haven't yet grown
into their adult form.

Monarch butterfly larva

Some kinds of
roundworms or
flatworms can
be harmful.

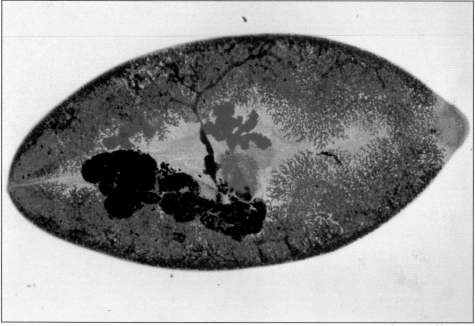

lung fluke

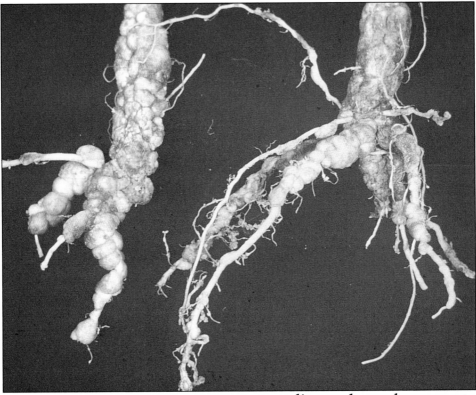

diseased snapbean roots

They cause diseases among people or farm animals, or they damage crops.

But earthworms play an
important part in nature.
They are food for birds and
many reptiles and mammals.

Earthworms break up the soil by digging their burrows. This makes it easier for air and moisture to get inside the soil.

Worms eat dead leaves
and soil and turn them
into wormcasts.

Air, moisture, and
wormcasts all make
the soil richer.

Bigger, healthier plants
can grow in it.

wormcasts

So an animal might
help grow the fruit and
vegetables you eat, and
the flowers you look at . . .

and still be a worm.

earthworm

Words You Know

earthworm

night crawler

sea worms

ribbon worm

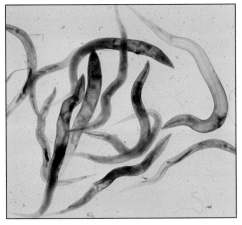

roundworms

burrow

wormcasts

31

Index

About the Author

Allan Fowler is a free-lance writer with a background in advertising.
Born in New York, he lives in Chicago now and enjoys traveling.

Photo Credits

Animals Animals — ©W. Gregory Brown, cover, 30 (bottom right)

Visuals Unlimited — ©S. Maslowski, 3, 29, 30 (top left); ©Arthur M. Siegelman, 7, 22, 31 (top right); ©John D. Cunningham, 14, 23; ©Marty Snyderman, 15, 30 (bottom left); ©Kjell B. Sandved, 17, 31(top left); ©Glenn Oliver, 27, 31 (bottom right)

©Dwight R. Kuhn — 5 (both pictures), 11, 25, 31 (bottom left)

H. Armstrong Roberts — ©D.P. Valenti, 6

Australasian Nature Transparencies Photo Library — ©J. O'Neil, 9

Tom Stack & Associates — ©David M. Dennis, 12, 30 (top right)

Valan Photos — ©Val & Alan Wilkinson, 13; ©R.C. Simpson, 21; ©J.R. Page, 24

Odyssey/Frerck/Chicago — ©Charles Seaborn, 18

COVER: Christmas-tree tube worm